Bond *ing*

The Power of Investing in Bonds

HENDRITH VANLON SMITH JR

Bond ing: The Power of Investing in Bonds

© 2024 Hendrith Vanlon Smith Jr. All Rights Reserved.

Published Independently.

No portion of this book may be put in or stored in a large language model or Artificial Intelligence system, except as permitted under section 107 or 108 of the 1976 United States Copyright Act, without written permission of the publisher or author.

Individuals and entities have the authors permission to distribute exact quotes from this book, given that the author is credited by name attached to the quote.

ISBN: 978-1-300-99150-2

Copies stored in The Library of Congress.

For rights and permissions, see Library of Congress registration.

Printed in The United States of America.

Contents

Introduction: 7
    The Bridge to Prosperity 7
    A Global Investor's Perspective 7
    Permaculture Investing: A Sustainable Approach 8
    An Invitation to Partnership and Learning 9

Part I: 11

The Fundamentals of Bonds 11

Chapter 1: What Are Bonds? 13
    Bonds: The Bedrock of Investment 13
    The Bond Triad: Government, Corporate, Municipal 15
    The Tapestry of Governance: How Government Structure Influences Municipal Bond Landscapes 21
    Decoding Bond Terminology 24
    PER ITEM EXAMPLES 25
    COMPREHENSIVE SCENARIO: 26
    Diving Deeper into the Nuances of the Bond Market 31
    The Debt-Ownership Dichotomy: 31
    A Market of Immense Scale and Complexity: 32
    The Bond Market's Ripple Effect: 33
    The Evolving Bond Market 33
    The Bond Market in 2050: A Colossal Colossus 34
    The Supremacy of the Bondholder 37

Chapter 2: Why Invest in Bonds? 41
    The Allure of Bonds: Stability, Income, and Impact 41
    Bonds vs. Other Investment Options 42

Case Studies: Bonds in Action 43

Chapter 3: The Global Bond Market - A Vast Tapestry of Opportunities 45

The Titans of the Bond Arena 45

Developed vs. Emerging Markets: A World of Contrasts . 46

The Currency Conundrum: Taming the Exchange Rate Dragon 47

Part II: 49

Advanced Bond Investing Strategies 49

Chapter 4: Building a Bond Portfolio - A Symphony of Stability and Growth 51

Asset Allocation: The Cornerstone of Portfolio Construction 51

Permaculture Principles: Nurturing a Resilient Portfolio Ecosystem 52

Active vs. Passive Management: The Conductor's Baton . 53

Holding vs. Trading: The Art of Patience and Timing 54

Chapter 5: Analyzing Bond Investments - Navigating the Sea of Risk and Reward 57

Credit Analysis: Gauging the Issuer's Strength 57

Interest Rate Risk: The Tide's Unpredictable Flow 58

Socioeconomic Factors: The Winds of Change 59

Tools and Resources: The Navigator's Compass 59

Chapter 6: Bond Investing in a Changing World - Navigating the Tides of Uncertainty 61

Economic Cycles: The Rhythm of Growth and Contraction 61

Geopolitical Events: The Tremors that Shake the Market. 62

Inflation: The Silent Erosion of Value 63

Adapting to Market Changes: The Art of Flexibility........ 63

Part III: 65

The Impact of Bond Investments 65

Chapter 7: Bonds and Infrastructure Development - Building the Foundations of Progress 67

The Financial Lifeline of Infrastructure 67

The Unique Value-Add of Bonds.................................... 68

Case Studies: Bonds in Action... 69

Chapter 8: Bonds and Social Impact - Catalysts for a Better World.. 71

Green Bonds: Financing a Sustainable Future 71

Social Bonds: Empowering Communities...................... 72

Examples of Socially Responsible Bond Investments....... 72

The Future of Africa: Bonds as Tools for Rapid Growth .. 73

Bonds as Enablers of Reaching New Frontiers 74

Chapter 9: The Future of Bond Investing - Forging a Path to a Sustainable and Equitable World 77

ESG Investing: Aligning Values with Investments 77

Impact Investing: Measuring the Ripple Effect............... 78

Addressing Global Challenges: Bonds as Agents of Change 79

The Path Forward: A Shared Vision 80

Conclusion: Embark on a Voyage of Prosperity and Impact with Mayflower-Plymouth.. 81

A Call to Action: Partner with Mayflower-Plymouth....... 81

The Power of Bonds: A Force for Good.......................... 82

Bond ing: The Power of Investing in Bonds

Introduction:

The Bridge to Prosperity

In the heart of Rwanda, amidst rolling hills and vibrant communities, lies a testament to the transformative power of bond investments. The Ruzizi III Hydropower Project, a marvel of engineering and collaboration, stands as a beacon of hope, illuminating a future where sustainable energy drives economic growth and empowers people's lives. This project, made possible through the collective investment of individuals and institutions across the globe, will provide clean, affordable electricity to millions of people – fueling industries, powering homes, and transforming communities.

This bridge, not only built of steel and concrete, but also of financial instruments and shared aspirations, exemplifies the profound impact that bond investments can have on a global scale. It underscores the interconnectedness of our world and the potential for capital to flow across borders, fostering progress and prosperity for all. That's the power of investing in Bonds!

A Global Investor's Perspective

I have dedicated years of my life to harnessing the power of bond investments to create wealth and drive positive change around the world. I think of myself as a Banker in the simplest sense of the word – one who provides capital. And as a Bond investor, that's what I do. As a globally recognized business and investment expert, I have witnessed firsthand the transformative potential of bonds, not only as a means of generating consistent returns but also as a catalyst for sustainable development and social progress.

Through my firm, I have experienced great success, navigating the complexities of the global bond market with expertise and precision. We have built a reputation for delivering exceptional results, even in the face of challenging economic climates, and we have done so while adhering to the principles of Permaculture Investing.

Permaculture Investing: A Sustainable Approach

Permaculture Investing is a philosophy that draws inspiration from the principles of permaculture, a design system that seeks to create sustainable and self-sufficient ecosystems. In the context of investing, it emphasizes the importance of long-term thinking, holistic diversification, and resilience.

By adopting a Permaculture Investing approach, we seek to create investment portfolios that are not only profitable but also contribute to the health and well-being of our planet and its inhabitants. We believe that by aligning our investments with the principles of sustainability and social responsibility, we can generate long-term returns, consistent income, and resilient growth for our partners.

An Invitation to Partnership and Learning

This book, "Bond ing: The Power of Investing in Bonds" is an invitation to potential partners. For those seeking to grow their wealth and make a positive impact on the world, I offer a unique opportunity to partner with a seasoned expert and tap into the vast potential of the global bond market with Mayflower-Plymouth.

Together, we will explore the transformative power of bonds, unlocking opportunities for financial success and sustainable development. This book will equip you with the basic knowledge and insights to understand the global bond market.

Join me on this journey as we discover the power of bonds, not only as a financial instrument but also as a force for good in the world.

Part I:

The Fundamentals of Bonds

Chapter 1: What Are Bonds?

Bonds: The Bedrock of Investment

Imagine you're lending money to a friend or family member. They promise to pay you back the amount you lent them, plus a little extra for your kindness. In the world of finance, this act of lending is formalized through an instrument called a *bond*. In essence, a bond is a loan you make to an entity—be it a government, a corporation, or a municipality—in exchange for regular interest payments and the return of your principal investment at a specified future date.

Picture this: Your niece (or cousin) Sarah, an aspiring entrepreneur, approaches you with a gleam in her eye and a business plan in hand. She needs a little seed money to get her artisanal bakery off the ground. You believe in her passion and potential, so you lend her a thousand dollars, with the understanding that she'll pay you back in full within two years, along with a little something extra each month to show her appreciation for your support.

That "little something extra" is akin to the interest you earn on a bond. In the grand theater of finance, a bond formalizes this friendly loan into a structured investment. You, the investor, become the lender, extending a financial lifeline to an entity in need of capital. This entity could be your local government looking to build a new school, a corporation aiming to expand its operations, or even a sovereign nation striving to bolster its infrastructure.

In return for your investment, the bond issuer promises to repay you the principal amount (the original sum you lent) at a predetermined maturity date. But that's not all. They also commit to paying you periodic interest payments, known as coupon payments, throughout the bond's life. It's like receiving a steady stream of "thank you" notes from your cousin Sarah, filled with gratitude and a small token of her appreciation for your belief in her dream.

Just as you trust Sarah to honor her commitment, bond investors rely on the issuer's creditworthiness—their ability to repay the debt. This trust is built on a foundation of financial strength, transparency, and a proven track record. Of course, the world of finance is not without its risks, and bond issuers, like any borrower, can face challenges. But by carefully assessing the issuer's creditworthiness and diversifying your bond investments, you can mitigate these risks and enjoy the rewards of stable income and capital preservation.

Bonds, in essence, represent a powerful partnership between investors and issuers, a symbiotic relationship that fuels economic growth, empowers dreams, and builds a brighter future for all. They are the financial threads that weave together the fabric of our society, connecting individuals, communities, and nations in a shared pursuit of progress and prosperity.

The Bond Triad: Government, Corporate, Municipal

Just as there are different types of borrowers in our personal lives, there are also different types of bond issuers in the financial world. (Think of issuing a bond as a formal way of asking for a loan.)

1. **Government Bonds (National Government)**: When a national government needs to raise funds for its various activities—be it building infrastructure, funding social programs, or managing its debt—it turns to the bond market. It issues government bonds, essentially borrowing money from investors in exchange for regular interest payments and the promise to repay the principal at maturity.

   These bonds are widely regarded as the safest type of bond investment. The reason? They're backed by the full faith and credit of the issuing government. This means that the government has the power to levy taxes and generate revenue to meet its debt obligations. In essence, you're lending money to an entity with the ultimate power to collect funds to repay you.

In the United States, these government bonds are known as Treasury bonds, or simply "Treasuries." They are issued by the U.S. Department of the Treasury and are considered virtually risk-free. This is because the U.S. government has never defaulted on its debt in its history, and it has the world's largest economy and taxing power to back its commitments.

The safety of government bonds makes them a cornerstone of many investment portfolios, particularly for those seeking capital preservation and stable income. They offer a reliable stream of interest payments and the assurance that your principal will be returned at maturity.

However, it's important to note that even government bonds are not entirely without risk. Inflation can erode the purchasing power of their fixed interest payments over time. Moreover, in rare cases, governments can face fiscal challenges or political instability that could impact their ability to repay their debt. And not all governments are created equal from a creditworthiness perspective.

Nevertheless, government bonds remain a vital component of the global bond market, providing a safe haven for investors and a crucial source of financing for governments worldwide. They serve as a benchmark for other interest rates and play a critical role in maintaining financial stability and promoting economic growth.

2. **Corporate Bonds**: When a company has ambitious plans - be it launching a groundbreaking product, expanding into new markets, or acquiring a rival firm - it often requires a substantial infusion of capital. To secure this funding, they may turn to the bond market, issuing corporate bonds to investors.

   Think of it as a company taking out a loan from the public. In exchange for the funds provided by investors, the company promises to pay regular interest payments (the coupon rate) and return the principal amount at a specified maturity date. However, unlike a bank loan with a single lender, a corporate bond is essentially sliced into numerous smaller loans, each represented by a bond certificate held by an investor. In a way, its like crowdfunding.

   The allure of corporate bonds lies in their potential for higher interest rates compared to government bonds. Companies, unlike governments, cannot simply raise taxes to guarantee repayment. Therefore, they must offer a higher yield to entice investors to take on the additional risk associated with their financial health.

   This risk stems from the inherent volatility of the corporate world. A company's financial performance can fluctuate due to various factors, such as economic downturns, changes in consumer preferences, or disruptive technological advancements. If a company faces financial difficulties, it may struggle to meet its debt obligations, leading to a potential default on its bonds.

Furthermore, there's a fundamental difference in the revenue streams of companies and governments. Governments have the power to levy taxes, providing a relatively stable and predictable income source to back their bond payments. Companies, on the other hand, rely on sales and profits, which can be affected by market competition, economic cycles, and other external factors. This inherent uncertainty in a company's revenue stream adds to the risk profile of corporate bonds.

Despite the inherent risks, corporate bonds play a vital role in the global economy, providing companies with the capital they need to grow, innovate, and create jobs. For investors, they offer the potential for higher returns and diversification benefits, balancing the stability of government bonds with the growth potential of equities.

However, investing in corporate bonds requires careful analysis and due diligence. It's essential to assess the company's financial strength, industry outlook, and management quality before committing your capital. Diversification across different sectors and credit ratings can also help mitigate risk and enhance the stability of your bond portfolio.

In the ever-evolving landscape of bond investing, corporate bonds represent a dynamic and rewarding asset class. By understanding their unique characteristics, risks, and potential rewards, investors can harness their power to achieve their financial goals while supporting the engines of economic growth and innovation.

3. **Municipal Bonds (Local Government)**: When a local government or its agencies need to raise capital for essential public projects – think schools where future generations will learn and grow, hospitals that provide vital healthcare services, or roads that connect communities and facilitate commerce – they turn to the municipal bond market.

Municipal bonds, often referred to as "munis," are debt securities issued by these entities. By purchasing a muni bond, you essentially become a lender to your local community, providing the crucial funding needed to build and maintain the infrastructure that underpins our society. In return for your investment, you receive regular interest payments and the promise of full repayment of your principal at maturity.

One of the most attractive features of municipal bonds is their tax advantage. In many cases, the interest earned on these bonds is exempt from federal income tax, and it may also be exempt from state and local taxes if you reside in the state where the bond was issued. This tax exemption can significantly enhance your after-tax returns, making munis particularly appealing to investors in higher tax brackets.

Imagine the impact of investing in a municipal bond that funds the construction of a new school in your neighborhood. Not only are you contributing to the education of future generations, but you're also enjoying tax-efficient income that can help you achieve your financial goals. It's a win-win scenario, where your investment dollars work to build a stronger community while also bolstering your own financial well-being.

However, it's important to remember that municipal bonds are not without risks. The financial health of the issuing municipality or agency can impact its ability to repay its debt. Factors such as economic downturns, population changes, or mismanagement can affect a local government's revenue streams and creditworthiness.

Therefore, it's crucial to conduct thorough research and due diligence before investing in municipal bonds. Analyze the issuer's financial statements, credit ratings, and the specific project being funded. Diversification across different municipalities and project types can also help mitigate risk and enhance the stability of your bond portfolio.

Municipal bonds represent a unique opportunity to invest in your community and support projects that enhance the quality of life for all. By carefully selecting and managing your muni bond investments, you can enjoy tax-advantaged income, contribute to the betterment of society, and build a legacy of responsible and impactful investing.

The Tapestry of Governance: How Government Structure Influences Municipal Bond Landscapes

The issuance and dynamics of municipal bonds are intricately tied to the structure of the governing bodies behind them. Just as the DNA of an organism shapes its characteristics, a government's design profoundly influences the landscape of its municipal bond market.

Federalism: A Balancing Act

In federal systems like the United States, power is divided between a central government and constituent states or provinces. This division creates a multi-layered municipal bond market with varying degrees of risk and reward.

States, empowered with their own taxing authority and regulatory frameworks, issue bonds to finance projects within their jurisdictions. These bonds can vary significantly in credit quality, reflecting the fiscal health and economic strength of the issuing state. For instance, a bond issued by a state with a robust economy and prudent fiscal management will likely command a lower interest rate than one from a state facing financial challenges.

Local governments within these states, such as cities, counties, and school districts, also issue bonds to fund their own projects. These bonds typically carry a higher risk profile than state-level bonds, as their financial strength can be more susceptible to local economic conditions and demographic shifts.

Centralized Systems: A Unified Front

In contrast, countries with centralized governments, where power is concentrated at the national level, tend to have a more uniform municipal bond market. Local governments in these systems often rely heavily on central government funding and may have limited authority to issue their own bonds.

This can result in a less diverse municipal bond market with fewer opportunities for investors seeking exposure to specific regions or project types. However, the backing of the central government can enhance the creditworthiness of these bonds, potentially offering greater stability and lower risk.

Other Structures: A Spectrum of Possibilities

Beyond federal and centralized systems, a variety of other government structures exist, each with its unique implications for the municipal bond market.

- Confederations: In confederations, like Switzerland, power rests primarily with the constituent states, which retain a high degree of autonomy. This can lead to a fragmented municipal bond market with varying credit quality and regulatory frameworks across different states.

- Unitary States: In unitary states, like France, the central government holds ultimate authority, with local governments exercising powers delegated to them. This can result in a more centralized municipal bond market, with local government bonds often carrying the implicit backing of the central government.

The Interplay of Factors

While government structure plays a significant role, other factors also influence the municipal bond landscape. These include:

- Economic Conditions: The overall economic health of a country or region can impact the creditworthiness of municipal bond issuers and the demand for their bonds.

- Fiscal Policies: Tax policies, spending priorities, and debt management practices can shape the financial strength of local governments and their ability to access the bond market.

- Legal and Regulatory Frameworks: The legal and regulatory environment governing bond issuance and trading can influence investor confidence and market liquidity.

- Investor Appetite: The demand for municipal bonds, driven by factors such as tax advantages and risk appetite, can also shape the market landscape.

In conclusion, the structure of various governments intricately influences the municipal bond landscape, creating a tapestry of opportunities and challenges for investors. By understanding these nuances and carefully analyzing the specific characteristics of each bond issuer, investors can navigate this complex market with confidence and build a diversified portfolio that aligns with their financial goals and risk tolerance.

Decoding Bond Terminology

- **Coupon Rate:** This is the fixed interest rate that the bond issuer pays to the bondholder, usually semi-annually. Think of it as the 'rent' you receive for lending your money.

- **Maturity Date:** This is the date on which the bond issuer will repay the principal amount, also known as the face value or par value, to the bondholder. It's when you get your original loan back.

- **Yield:** While the coupon rate is fixed, the yield can fluctuate depending on the market price of the bond. If you buy a bond at a discount (below its face value), your yield will be higher than the coupon rate, and vice versa.

- **Credit Rating:** This is an assessment of the bond issuer's creditworthiness, indicating their ability to repay the debt. Higher-rated bonds are generally considered safer but offer lower yields.

PER ITEM EXAMPLES

1. Coupon Rate Example

- **Scenario:** You purchase a corporate bond with a face value of $1,000 and a coupon rate of 5%.

- **Explanation:** This means the company will pay you $50 in interest per year (5% of $1,000). Since most bonds pay interest semi-annually, you'll receive two payments of $25 each year.

2. Maturity Date Example

- **Scenario:** You buy a U.S. Treasury bond with a maturity date of 2030.

- **Explanation:** In the year 2030, the U.S. government will repay you the full face value of the bond (e.g., $1,000) in addition to any remaining interest payments.

3. Yield Example

- **Scenario:** A bond with a face value of $1,000 and a 4% coupon rate is currently trading at $950 in the market.

- **Explanation:** You're buying the bond at a discount. While the coupon rate remains 4%, your actual yield will be higher because you're paying less than the face value for the bond. The yield calculation takes into account the discount and the interest payments you'll receive until maturity.

COMPREHENSIVE SCENARIO:

Scenario:

You're considering investing in a municipal bond issued by the City of Orlando to fund a new park. The bond has the following features:

- **Face Value:** $1,000

- **Coupon Rate:** 3%

- **Maturity Date:** 2035
- **Credit Rating:** AA (High Quality)
- **Current Market Price:** $900

Explanation:

- **Coupon Rate:** The city will pay you $30 per year in interest (3% of $1,000), typically in two semi-annual payments of $15.

- **Maturity Date:** In the year 2035, the City of Orlando will repay you the full face value of $1,000, along with any final interest payment.

- **Yield:** Since you're buying the bond at a discount ($900 instead of $1,000), your yield will be higher than the 3% coupon rate. The exact yield will depend on how long it is until the bond matures, but it will be more than 3% because you're getting the $30 annual interest plus the $100 difference between what you paid and the face value you'll receive at maturity.

- **Credit Rating:** The AA rating indicates that the City of Orlando has a very strong capacity to meet its financial commitments. This suggests the bond is relatively safe, though not entirely risk-free.

Additional Considerations

- **Tax Advantages:** Municipal bonds often offer tax benefits, meaning the interest you earn may be exempt from federal, and possibly state and local, income taxes. This can further enhance your yield.

- **Market Fluctuations:** While the coupon rate and maturity date are fixed, the market price of the bond can change. If interest rates rise, the price of your bond could decrease. However, if you hold the bond until maturity, you'll still receive the full face value.

This example demonstrates how the different bond terminology concepts interact to influence your investment decision. Understanding these terms will empower you to evaluate bond opportunities and build a portfolio that aligns with your financial goals and risk tolerance.

Scenario:

Let's say Mayflower-Plymouth manages over $1 billion in assets. We are considering adding to our fixed-income portfolio with a bond issued by a major technology company, "TechCorp." This bond has the following characteristics:

- **Face Value:** $10,000,000

- **Coupon Rate:** 4.5%

- **Maturity Date:** 2040

- **Credit Rating:** A+ (Strong)

- **Current Market Price:** $9,700,000

Explanation and Considerations:

- **Investment Scale:** Unlike individual investors who might buy a single $1,000 bond, Mayflower-Plymouth operates at a much larger scale. We're considering purchasing $10 million worth of TechCorp bonds to make a meaningful impact on our portfolio.

- **Coupon Income:** With a 4.5% coupon rate on $10 million, TechCorp will pay Mayflower-Plymouth **$450,000 in interest annually**. This substantial income stream can be reinvested or used to meet other partnership obligations.

- **Maturity and Reinvestment Risk:** The bond matures in 2040. While we'll receive the $10 million face value back then, we need to consider what the prevailing interest rate environment might be. Will we be able to reinvest that principal at a similar or higher rate in 2040?

- **Yield and Market Conditions:** Since the bond is trading at a discount (below its face value), our yield will be higher than the 4.5% coupon rate. This is because we're paying $9.7 million for something that will pay back $10 million at maturity, plus the annual interest. However, bond prices fluctuate with interest rate changes. If interest rates rise significantly, the market value of our TechCorp bond could decline before maturity.

- **Credit Risk:** Though TechCorp has a strong A+ credit rating, there's always a risk that the company could face financial difficulties and default on its bond payments. Mayflower-Plymouth would need to assess this risk carefully, especially given the large investment amount.

- **Portfolio Diversification:** How does this TechCorp bond fit into our overall portfolio strategy? Are we overexposed to the technology sector? Does this bond provide the right balance of risk and return within our fixed-income allocation?

- **Liquidity:** While large institutional investors like Mayflower-Plymouth often have more access to bond markets, it's still important to consider the liquidity of this bond. Can we easily sell it if we need to access the capital before maturity?

Additional Factors for a Billion-Dollar Fund:

- **Benchmarking:** How does the potential return of this bond compare to our benchmark? Large funds often have performance targets to meet.

- **Economic Outlook:** Factor in our macroeconomic outlook. How might inflation, economic growth, and future interest rate changes impact the value of this bond?

Diving Deeper into the Nuances of the Bond Market

While the fundamental concepts of bonds—coupon rate, maturity date, yield, and credit rating—provide a solid foundation, the bond market is a vast and intricate landscape with unique characteristics that set it apart from the stock market.

The Debt-Ownership Dichotomy:

One of the most crucial distinctions lies in the nature of the investment itself. Stocks represent ownership in a company, granting shareholders a stake in its profits and growth potential. Bonds, on the other hand, represent debt. When you purchase a bond, you're essentially lending money to the issuer, who is obligated to repay you with interest.

This distinction has significant implications, particularly in the unfortunate event of bankruptcy. Bondholders, as creditors, have a higher claim on the issuer's assets than stockholders. In a liquidation scenario, bondholders are prioritized in the repayment hierarchy, increasing the likelihood of recovering at least a portion of their investment.

A Market of Immense Scale and Complexity:

The bond market dwarfs the stock market in terms of sheer size and complexity. It encompasses a staggering variety of bonds issued by governments, corporations, and municipalities across the globe. Each bond carries its own unique set of features, including:

- **Maturity:** Ranging from short-term bonds maturing in a few months to long-term bonds with maturities spanning decades.

- **Credit Rating:** From highly rated, low-risk bonds issued by stable governments to high-yield, higher-risk bonds issued by companies with less certain financial prospects.

- **Callability:** Some bonds can be redeemed by the issuer before their maturity date, potentially impacting an investor's expected returns.

- **Convertibility:** Certain bonds offer the option to convert into a predetermined number of the issuer's shares, blending debt and equity features.

Navigating this vast and diverse market requires a deep understanding of its intricacies. Investors must carefully consider their risk tolerance, investment goals, and the prevailing economic environment to construct a bond portfolio that aligns with their needs.

The Bond Market's Ripple Effect:

The bond market plays a pivotal role in the global economy. It provides a vital source of capital for governments and corporations, enabling them to fund infrastructure projects, expand operations, and pursue innovation. Bond yields also serve as benchmarks for other interest rates, influencing borrowing costs for businesses and consumers alike.

Moreover, the bond market acts as a barometer of investor sentiment and economic health. Fluctuations in bond prices and yields can signal shifts in market expectations and provide valuable insights into the future direction of the economy.

In conclusion, the bond market is a dynamic and multifaceted arena that offers a wealth of opportunities for discerning investors. By delving deeper into its complexities and understanding its unique nuances, you can unlock its full potential and build a resilient and rewarding bond portfolio.

The Evolving Bond Market

The bond market is not static; it constantly evolves in response to economic conditions, technological advancements, and regulatory changes. Some of the upcoming changes and trends to watch for include:

- **The Rise of ESG Bonds:** Environmental, Social, and Governance (ESG) bonds are gaining traction as investors increasingly seek to align their portfolios with their values.

- **Technological Innovation:** Blockchain technology and artificial intelligence are being explored to streamline bond issuance and trading, potentially increasing efficiency and transparency.

- **Regulatory Changes:** The regulatory landscape for bonds is constantly evolving, impacting everything from issuance to trading practices. Staying abreast of these changes is crucial for bond investors.

In conclusion, bonds are a fundamental building block of any well-diversified investment portfolio. By understanding the different types of bonds, key terminology, and the evolving nature of the bond market, you can make informed investment decisions and harness the power of bonds to achieve your financial goals.

The Bond Market in 2050: A Colossal Colossus

The global bond market, already a behemoth dwarfing its equity counterpart, is poised for unprecedented growth in the coming decades. By 2050, this financial colossus is projected to reach staggering proportions, fueled by a confluence of factors that will reshape the investment landscape and create a wealth of opportunities for discerning investors.

While precise forecasts are elusive, experts predict that the global bond market could swell to over $200 trillion by 2050. This exponential expansion will be driven by several key trends:

1. **Rising Global Debt:** As governments and corporations grapple with mounting fiscal challenges and infrastructure needs, they will increasingly turn to the bond market for financing. The International Monetary Fund (IMF) projects that global debt will continue to rise, reaching unprecedented levels in the coming decades. This surge in debt issuance will fuel the growth of the bond market, providing ample opportunities for investors.

2. **Aging Demographics:** The world's population is aging rapidly, with a growing proportion of retirees seeking stable income and capital preservation. Bonds, with their predictable cash flows and lower volatility compared to stocks, will become increasingly attractive to this demographic, driving demand and expanding the market.

3. **Infrastructure Investment Boom:** The world faces a massive infrastructure deficit, estimated at trillions of dollars. To bridge this gap, governments and private entities will rely heavily on bond financing to fund critical projects in transportation, energy, and telecommunications. This infrastructure investment boom will further propel the growth of the bond market.

4. **Sustainable Investing Surge:** The rise of ESG investing and impact investing will continue to reshape the bond market, with a growing emphasis on green bonds, social bonds, and sustainability-linked bonds. This trend will attract a new wave of investors seeking to align their financial goals with their values, further expanding the market.

5. **Technological Innovation:** Advancements in financial technology, such as blockchain and artificial intelligence, will streamline bond issuance and trading, enhancing efficiency, transparency, and accessibility. This will likely attract new investors and deepen market participation.

The bond market in 2050 will be a vastly different landscape than it is today. It will be larger, more diverse, and more accessible, offering a plethora of opportunities for investors seeking stability, income, and impact.

However, this growth will also bring new challenges. Increased complexity, heightened competition, and evolving regulatory frameworks will require investors to adapt their strategies and stay ahead of the curve.

As we navigate this exciting future, let us embrace the potential of the bond market to create wealth, drive progress, and build a more sustainable and equitable world. The journey ahead is filled with promise, and by harnessing the power of bonds, we can shape a brighter future for ourselves and generations to come.

The Supremacy of the Bondholder

In the tumultuous landscape of corporate finance, where fortunes can rise and fall with the tides of the market, one principle remains steadfast: the supremacy of the bondholder. This principle, enshrined in bankruptcy laws and financial practices worldwide, dictates that in the event of a company's insolvency or bankruptcy, bondholders take precedence over stockholders in the repayment hierarchy. This prioritization stems from the fundamental nature of bonds as debt instruments, representing a legal obligation for the issuer to repay the borrowed principal along with interest.

The Legal Framework

The legal underpinnings of the bondholder's supremacy are deeply rooted in contract law and bankruptcy statutes. When a company issues bonds, it enters into a binding contract with the bondholders, outlining the terms of the loan, including the interest rate, maturity date, and repayment schedule. This contract establishes a creditor-debtor relationship, granting bondholders a legal claim on the issuer's assets in case of default.

Bankruptcy laws further solidify this hierarchy by establishing a clear order of priority for distributing the company's remaining assets to its various claimants. Secured creditors, such as those holding bonds backed by specific collateral, are typically first in line, followed by unsecured creditors, including bondholders without specific collateral. Stockholders, representing ownership in the company, are relegated to the bottom of the pecking order, receiving any residual value only after all creditor claims have been satisfied.

Rationale and Effects

The rationale behind this prioritization is twofold. Firstly, it provides a degree of protection to bondholders, who are essentially lenders to the company. By granting them a higher claim on the issuer's assets, it incentivizes them to provide capital, knowing that their investment is relatively secure even in the face of financial distress. Secondly, it promotes stability in the financial markets by ensuring that debt obligations are honored, fostering confidence among investors and lenders.

The effects of this principle are far-reaching. It influences the pricing of bonds, with riskier issuers having to offer higher interest rates to compensate bondholders for the increased risk of default. It also shapes the behavior of companies, encouraging them to maintain sound financial practices and avoid excessive leverage to minimize the risk of bankruptcy.

For bond investors, the supremacy of the bondholder provides a crucial layer of security, enabling them to participate in the growth of companies and economies while mitigating the downside risks associated with financial distress. It underscores the power of bonds as a reliable and resilient investment vehicle, capable of generating consistent returns and weathering market storms.

Chapter 2: Why Invest in Bonds?

The Allure of Bonds: Stability, Income, and Impact

In the dynamic world of investing, where market fluctuations and uncertainties abound, bonds emerge as a beacon of stability and resilience. They offer a compelling combination of benefits that make them an indispensable component of any well-rounded investment portfolio. Let's delve into the key advantages that make bonds an attractive investment option.

1. Stable Income Stream

One of the primary attractions of bonds is their ability to generate a predictable and consistent income stream. The coupon payments, paid semi-annually or annually, provide a reliable source of cash flow that can be used to meet living expenses, reinvest in other opportunities, or simply enhance your financial security. This steady income stream is particularly appealing to retirees or those seeking a dependable source of passive income.

2. Diversification Powerhouse

Bonds play a crucial role in diversifying your investment portfolio. Their low correlation with stocks means that when the stock market experiences volatility, bonds tend to hold their value or even appreciate. This diversification helps to reduce the overall risk of your portfolio, providing a buffer against market downturns and enhancing its long-term stability.

3. Safe Haven in Turbulent Times

Bonds, especially government bonds issued by financially stable countries, are often considered a safe haven asset. In times of economic uncertainty or market turmoil, investors flock to bonds, seeking refuge from the volatility of stocks and other riskier assets. This flight to safety can drive up bond prices and lower their yields, further reinforcing their role as a stabilizing force in your portfolio.

4. Benefits to Society

Beyond their financial benefits, bond investments can also contribute to the betterment of society. When you invest in bonds, you're essentially providing capital to governments, corporations, and municipalities to fund essential projects and initiatives. These can range from infrastructure development, such as building roads, bridges, and schools, to financing renewable energy projects and social impact initiatives. By investing in bonds, you become a part of the solution, supporting projects that enhance the quality of life for communities and contribute to a more sustainable future.

Bonds vs. Other Investment Options

While bonds offer a compelling array of benefits, it's essential to understand how they compare to other popular investment options like stocks and real estate.

- **Bonds vs. Stocks:** Stocks offer the potential for higher returns but also come with greater volatility and risk. Bonds, on the other hand, provide more stable returns and lower risk, making them ideal for investors seeking income and capital preservation.

- **Bonds vs. Real Estate:** Real estate investments can offer diversification and potential for appreciation, but they also come with higher transaction costs, illiquidity, and management challenges. Bonds provide greater liquidity and easier access to your investment.

Case Studies: Bonds in Action

To illustrate the power of bond investments, let's look at a couple of real-world examples:

1. **The Ruzizi III Hydropower Project**: This landmark project, funded in part by bond investments, is set to provide clean energy to millions in East Africa, driving economic growth and improving lives.

2. **U.S. Treasury Bonds during the 2008 Financial Crisis**: As the stock market plunged during the 2008 crisis, U.S. Treasury bonds soared in value, providing a safe haven for investors and demonstrating their resilience in turbulent times.

These examples highlight the diverse ways in which bond investments can create value, both financially and socially. By incorporating bonds into your portfolio, you can achieve a balance of stability, income, and impact, setting yourself on a path to long-term financial success while contributing to a better world.

Chapter 3: The Global Bond Market - A Vast Tapestry of Opportunities

The global bond market, an intricate network of interconnected financial flows, stands as a testament to human ingenuity and the relentless pursuit of progress. Spanning continents and currencies, this colossal market, valued at over $128 trillion, dwarfs its equity counterpart, offering a vast tapestry of opportunities for discerning investors. Let's embark on a journey through this dynamic landscape, exploring its key players, regional nuances, and the ever-present currency risk.

The Titans of the Bond Arena

Within the global bond market, a cast of formidable players orchestrates the symphony of debt and investment. National governments, multinational corporations, and supranational institutions like the World Bank and the International Monetary Fund all issue bonds to finance their operations and aspirations. Institutional investors, such as pension funds, insurance companies, and sovereign wealth funds, channel vast sums of capital into these bonds, seeking stable returns and diversification.

Central banks, the guardians of monetary policy, also wield significant influence in the bond market. Through their open market operations, they can buy or sell bonds to manage interest rates and stimulate or cool down economies. Their actions reverberate throughout the market, shaping yields and influencing investment decisions.

Developed vs. Emerging Markets: A World of Contrasts

The global bond market is a mosaic of diverse regions, each with its own unique characteristics and investment dynamics. Developed markets, such as the United States, Europe, and Japan, boast deep and liquid bond markets with established regulatory frameworks and transparent pricing mechanisms. These markets offer a haven of stability and predictability, attracting investors seeking safety and consistent returns.

Emerging markets, on the other hand, present a more adventurous terrain, characterized by higher growth potential but also elevated risks. Countries like Brazil, India, and China, with their burgeoning economies and expanding infrastructure needs, offer enticing opportunities for yield-hungry investors. However, these markets can also be volatile, susceptible to political instability, currency fluctuations, and economic shocks.

Navigating these contrasting landscapes requires a keen understanding of each region's economic fundamentals, political climate, and regulatory environment. A successful global bond investor must possess a discerning eye, capable of identifying hidden gems amidst the complexities and uncertainties of emerging markets, while also appreciating the steady virtues of developed markets.

The Currency Conundrum: Taming the Exchange Rate Dragon

Investing in bonds denominated in foreign currencies introduces an additional layer of complexity: currency risk. The value of your investment can fluctuate depending on the exchange rate between the foreign currency and your home currency. A depreciation of the foreign currency can erode your returns, even if the bond itself performs well.

To mitigate currency risk, astute investors employ a range of strategies. Hedging, through the use of currency derivatives, can lock in exchange rates and protect against adverse movements. Diversification across multiple currencies can also reduce the impact of any single currency's fluctuations. Moreover, a deep understanding of global macroeconomic trends and their potential impact on exchange rates is essential for navigating this treacherous terrain.

In conclusion, the global bond market is a vast and dynamic arena, teeming with opportunities and challenges. By embracing its complexities, understanding its regional nuances, and skillfully managing currency risk, investors can unlock its full potential and build a resilient and rewarding bond portfolio that spans the globe.

As we continue our journey through the world of bond investing, let us remember that this market is not merely a collection of financial instruments but a reflection of human aspirations, economic progress, and the interconnectedness of our world.

Part II:

Advanced Bond Investing Strategies

Chapter 4: Building a Bond Portfolio - A Symphony of Stability and Growth

Constructing a robust bond portfolio is akin to cultivating a thriving ecosystem, where each element plays a crucial role in maintaining balance, resilience, and long-term prosperity. By embracing the principles of Permaculture Investing, we can create a harmonious blend of bonds that generate consistent income, preserve capital, and foster sustainable growth. Let's delve into the art and science of building a bond portfolio that stands the test of time.

Asset Allocation: The Cornerstone of Portfolio Construction

Asset allocation, the strategic distribution of your investments across different asset classes, serves as the bedrock of your portfolio's architecture. For bond investors, this involves determining the optimal mix of bonds, stocks, and other assets based on your risk tolerance, investment goals, and time horizon.

A conservative investor nearing retirement might favor a higher allocation to bonds, seeking stability and income preservation. A younger investor with a longer time horizon might opt for a more aggressive allocation, including a greater proportion of equities for potential growth.

Permaculture Principles: Nurturing a Resilient Portfolio Ecosystem

Permaculture Investing, a philosophy inspired by the principles of permaculture, offers a valuable framework for building a sustainable and resilient bond portfolio.

- **Diversity:** Just as a diverse ecosystem is more resistant to shocks and disturbances, a diversified bond portfolio can weather market fluctuations and economic downturns. This involves diversifying across bond types (government, corporate, municipal), maturities (short-term, intermediate-term, long-term), and regions (developed and emerging markets).

- **Resilience:** A resilient portfolio is designed to withstand unforeseen events and adapt to changing conditions. This can be achieved through careful selection of bonds with varying credit ratings, maturities, and interest rate sensitivities.

- **Sustainability:** Permaculture Investing emphasizes the importance of aligning investments with long-term sustainability goals. This can involve incorporating green bonds, social impact bonds, or other instruments that support environmental and social progress.

Active vs. Passive Management: The Conductor's Baton

The choice between active and passive bond investing is akin to deciding whether to conduct an orchestra or simply enjoy the symphony. Active management involves actively buying and selling bonds in an attempt to outperform the market. This requires in-depth research, analysis, and a keen understanding of market dynamics.

Passive management, on the other hand, involves tracking a bond index and replicating its performance. This approach offers lower costs and simplicity but may sacrifice the potential for outperformance. The optimal choice depends on your investment philosophy, risk tolerance, and the resources available to you.

In my humble opinion, success in the future will require both active and passive – and, what I call "the active management of passive." Passive instruments like ETF's offer many benefits and should be included in a bond portfolio. At the same time, new opportunities will be emerging in an ever-changing world – many of those new opportunities will be coming out of African nations, companies in new industries, and risky infrastructure projects, some of which may be on other planets. Visionary bankers will only be able to capitalize greatly on these opportunities through active investing.

Holding vs. Trading: The Art of Patience and Timing

In the bond market, patience can be as rewarding as timing. Holding bonds to maturity allows you to collect all coupon payments and receive the full face value at maturity, regardless of market fluctuations. This "buy-and-hold" strategy offers predictability and stability, particularly for those seeking income.

Trading bonds, on the other hand, involves buying and selling them before maturity to capitalize on price movements and interest rate changes. This approach requires active management and market acumen, but it can potentially generate higher returns.

The ideal strategy depends on your investment objectives and risk appetite. A balanced approach, combining both holding and trading, can offer a blend of stability and potential for capital appreciation.

In conclusion, building a successful bond portfolio is a dynamic and ongoing process that requires careful planning, diversification, and a commitment to long-term sustainability. By embracing the principles of Permaculture Investing and adopting a disciplined approach, you can create a bond portfolio that not only generates consistent income and preserves capital but also contributes to a more prosperous and sustainable future. Remember, the bond market is not just a collection of financial instruments; it's a reflection of our collective aspirations, a testament to human ingenuity, and a powerful tool for shaping a better world.

Chapter 5: Analyzing Bond Investments - Navigating the Sea of Risk and Reward

In the intricate world of bond investing, where fortunes are built on informed decisions and prudent risk management, the ability to analyze bond investments with precision and foresight is paramount. Let's embark on a voyage through the key facets of bond analysis, exploring creditworthiness, interest rate risk, socioeconomic factors, and the invaluable tools that empower investors to make sound choices.

Credit Analysis: Gauging the Issuer's Strength

The bedrock of bond analysis lies in assessing the creditworthiness of the bond issuer. Just as a lender scrutinizes a borrower's financial health before extending a loan, bond investors must carefully evaluate the issuer's ability to meet its debt obligations. This involves delving into the issuer's financial statements, cash flow projections, and overall economic outlook.

Credit rating agencies, such as Standard & Poor's, Moody's, and Fitch, provide valuable insights into an issuer's creditworthiness through their rating systems. These ratings, ranging from AAA (highest quality) to D (default), offer a standardized assessment of credit risk, aiding investors in making informed decisions.

However, relying solely on credit ratings can be perilous. Astute investors go beyond the ratings, conducting their own due diligence and considering factors such as the issuer's industry, competitive landscape, and management quality. By adopting a holistic approach to credit analysis, you can uncover hidden risks and opportunities, ensuring your bond investments are built on a solid foundation.

Interest Rate Risk: The Tide's Unpredictable Flow

Interest rate risk, the potential for bond prices to fluctuate in response to changes in prevailing interest rates, is a constant companion for bond investors. When interest rates rise, the value of existing bonds tends to decline, as their fixed coupon payments become less attractive compared to newly issued bonds with higher yields. Conversely, when interest rates fall, existing bonds with higher coupon rates become more valuable, potentially leading to capital appreciation.

The duration of a bond, a measure of its sensitivity to interest rate changes, plays a crucial role in managing this risk. Bonds with longer durations are more susceptible to interest rate fluctuations, while shorter-duration bonds offer greater stability. By carefully balancing the duration of your bond portfolio, you can mitigate interest rate risk and navigate the ever-changing tides of the market.

Socioeconomic Factors: The Winds of Change

Beyond creditworthiness and interest rate risk, socioeconomic factors can also exert a profound influence on bond investments. Economic growth, inflation, geopolitical events, and demographic shifts can all impact the performance of bonds and shape the investment landscape.

For instance, a booming economy might lead to rising interest rates and lower bond prices, while a recession could trigger a flight to safety, driving up bond prices and lowering yields. Inflation erodes the purchasing power of fixed coupon payments, making inflation-protected bonds an attractive option. Geopolitical tensions can create uncertainty and volatility in certain regions, impacting the value of bonds issued by those countries.

Staying abreast of these socioeconomic trends and their potential impact on bond markets is crucial for successful investing. By incorporating these factors into your analysis, you can anticipate market movements and make informed decisions that align with your investment goals.

Tools and Resources: The Navigator's Compass

In the digital age, a wealth of tools and resources are available to aid bond investors in their quest for knowledge and insight. Financial news outlets, online brokerages, and specialized bond research platforms provide a constant stream of data, analysis, and commentary on the bond market.

Furthermore, sophisticated financial models and analytical tools can help you evaluate bond valuations, assess interest rate risk, and construct optimized portfolios. By leveraging these resources and honing your analytical skills, you can navigate the complexities of the bond market with confidence and clarity.

In conclusion, analyzing bond investments requires a multi-faceted approach that encompasses credit analysis, interest rate risk management, and a keen awareness of socioeconomic factors. By diligently employing the tools and resources at your disposal, you can gain a deeper understanding of the bond market's dynamics and make informed decisions that lead to long-term success. Remember, the bond market is not just a collection of financial instruments; it's a reflection of the world's economic pulse, a testament to human resilience, and a powerful tool for shaping a more prosperous future.

Chapter 6: Bond Investing in a Changing World - Navigating the Tides of Uncertainty

The global bond market, a vast and intricate web of interconnected financial flows, is perpetually in flux, shaped by the ebb and flow of economic cycles, the tremors of geopolitical events, and the relentless march of inflation. As astute investors, we must not only understand these forces but also adapt our strategies to navigate the ever-shifting tides of uncertainty. In this chapter, we will explore the profound impact of these factors on bond markets and equip ourselves with the tools to thrive in this dynamic landscape.

Economic Cycles: The Rhythm of Growth and Contraction

Economic cycles, the natural fluctuations of economic activity characterized by periods of expansion and contraction, exert a profound influence on bond markets. During periods of economic growth, businesses thrive, consumer spending rises, and interest rates tend to increase. This environment can lead to lower bond prices, as investors seek higher yields in other asset classes.

Conversely, during economic downturns, businesses struggle, unemployment rises, and central banks often lower interest rates to stimulate the economy. This can create a favorable environment for bond investors, as lower interest rates drive up bond prices and increase their appeal as a safe haven asset.

Understanding the current phase of the economic cycle and anticipating its potential trajectory is crucial for bond investors. By aligning their investment strategies with the prevailing economic winds, they can position their portfolios for success and capitalize on opportunities that arise during both boom and bust cycles.

Geopolitical Events: The Tremors that Shake the Market

Geopolitical events, such as wars, elections, and policy changes, can send shockwaves through the global bond market. Political instability or heightened tensions can trigger a flight to safety, driving investors towards bonds issued by stable and secure countries. This can lead to a divergence in yields, with bonds from troubled regions experiencing higher yields to compensate for increased risk.

Conversely, positive geopolitical developments, such as peace agreements or trade deals, can boost investor confidence and lead to lower bond yields across the board. The interconnectedness of the global economy means that events in one corner of the world can have ripple effects on bond markets far and wide.

Staying informed about geopolitical developments and their potential impact on bond markets is essential for navigating this complex landscape. By understanding the interplay between politics and finance, investors can anticipate market reactions and adjust their strategies accordingly.

Inflation: The Silent Erosion of Value

Inflation, the gradual increase in the general price level of goods and services, poses a significant challenge for bond investors. As inflation rises, the purchasing power of fixed coupon payments diminishes, eroding the real returns on bond investments.

To combat this silent erosion of value, investors can turn to inflation-protected bonds, such as Treasury Inflation-Protected Securities (TIPS) in the United States. These bonds offer a coupon rate that adjusts with inflation, providing a hedge against rising prices and preserving the purchasing power of your investment.

Adapting to Market Changes: The Art of Flexibility

In the ever-changing world of bond investing, adaptability is key. Market conditions can shift rapidly, and unforeseen events can disrupt even the most carefully laid plans. To thrive in this dynamic environment, investors must be willing to adjust their strategies, rebalance their portfolios, and seize new opportunities as they arise.

This might involve shifting allocations between different bond types, maturities, or regions based on the prevailing economic and geopolitical climate. It could also entail actively managing your bond portfolio, buying and selling bonds to capitalize on market movements and interest rate changes.

The key is to remain informed, vigilant, and flexible, always ready to adapt your strategies to the ever-evolving landscape of the bond market. By embracing change and navigating its currents with skill and confidence, you can achieve long-term success in the world of bond investing.

Part III:

The Impact of Bond Investments

Bond ing: The Power of Investing in Bonds

Chapter 7: Bonds and Infrastructure Development - Building the Foundations of Progress

In the grand tapestry of human civilization, infrastructure stands as the backbone of progress, connecting communities, fostering economic growth, and enhancing the quality of life for all. From the majestic bridges that span mighty rivers to the intricate networks of roads that crisscross continents, infrastructure projects embody our collective aspirations and our unwavering commitment to building a better future.

But these ambitious undertakings require substantial capital, often beyond the immediate reach of governments and private entities. This is where bond investments emerge as a powerful catalyst, channeling the collective savings of individuals and institutions into the very foundations of progress. Let us explore the profound impact of bond investments on infrastructure development and the unique value they bring to these transformative projects.

The Financial Lifeline of Infrastructure

Infrastructure projects, by their very nature, are capital-intensive endeavors. They require massive investments in materials, labor, and technology, often spanning several years or even decades.

Governments, with their limited budgets and competing priorities, often struggle to finance these projects solely through taxation or direct funding.

This is where bonds step in, providing a vital source of long-term financing. By issuing bonds, governments and public agencies can tap into the vast pool of capital available in the bond market, attracting investors seeking stable returns and a tangible impact on society. These bonds, backed by the full faith and credit of the issuer or the revenue generated by the project itself, offer investors a secure and predictable income stream while providing the necessary funds to bring infrastructure dreams to life.

The Unique Value-Add of Bonds

In the absence of bond financing, infrastructure projects would face significant hurdles and limitations. Governments might be forced to rely on short-term funding sources, such as bank loans or private equity, which can be more expensive and subject to greater volatility. This could lead to delays, cost overruns, and even the abandonment of crucial projects.

Bonds, with their long maturities and fixed interest rates, offer a stable and predictable source of financing that aligns with the long-term nature of infrastructure development. They enable governments to spread the cost of projects over several decades, making them more affordable and sustainable. Moreover, the transparency and regulatory oversight associated with bond issuance foster investor confidence and ensure that funds are used efficiently and responsibly.

Case Studies: Bonds in Action

The transformative power of bond investments in infrastructure development is evident in countless projects around the world. Let's explore a few inspiring examples:

- **The Golden Gate Bridge**: This iconic landmark, a testament to human engineering and ambition, was financed in part through the issuance of municipal bonds. These bonds, backed by tolls collected from bridge users, provided the necessary capital to complete this monumental project, which has become a symbol of San Francisco and a vital transportation artery for millions.

- **The Panama Canal Expansion**: The expansion of the Panama Canal, a marvel of modern engineering, was also made possible through bond financing. The Panama Canal Authority issued bonds to international investors, leveraging the canal's strategic importance and revenue potential to secure the necessary funds for this ambitious undertaking. The expanded canal now accommodates larger ships, boosting global trade and driving economic growth in the region.

- **India's Renewable Energy Boom**: India, a country committed to sustainable development, has harnessed the power of green bonds to finance its ambitious renewable energy goals. These bonds, issued by both public and private entities, have attracted significant investment from environmentally conscious investors, fueling the growth of solar and wind power projects across the country. This green energy revolution is not only reducing India's carbon footprint but also creating jobs, improving air quality, and enhancing energy security.

These examples, and countless others, illustrate the profound impact that bond investments can have on infrastructure development. By providing the financial fuel for these transformative projects, bonds empower communities, drive economic growth, and pave the way for a more sustainable and prosperous future.

As we continue our exploration of the bond market, let us remember that these investments are not just about generating returns; they are about building the foundations of progress, connecting people and places, and leaving a lasting legacy for generations to come.

Chapter 8: Bonds and Social Impact - Catalysts for a Better World

In an era where the pursuit of profit is increasingly intertwined with the quest for purpose, bonds are emerging as powerful instruments for driving positive social change. Beyond their traditional role as financial instruments, bonds are now being harnessed to finance projects that address pressing environmental and social challenges, from combating climate change to promoting affordable housing and expanding access to education. In this chapter, we will explore the transformative potential of bonds as catalysts for social impact and envision a future where finance serves as a force for good.

Green Bonds: Financing a Sustainable Future

Green bonds, a rapidly growing segment of the bond market, are specifically designed to finance projects that promote environmental sustainability. These bonds, issued by governments, corporations, and financial institutions, channel capital into initiatives such as renewable energy, energy efficiency, clean transportation, and sustainable water management.

By investing in green bonds, individuals and institutions can actively contribute to the fight against climate change and the transition to a low-carbon economy. These bonds offer a compelling opportunity to align financial goals with environmental values, demonstrating that responsible investing can be both profitable and impactful.

Social Bonds: Empowering Communities

Social bonds, another innovative category of impact bonds, focus on addressing social challenges and improving the lives of underserved communities. These bonds finance projects that promote affordable housing, healthcare, education, and economic development, particularly in disadvantaged regions.

By investing in social bonds, individuals and institutions can play a direct role in creating a more equitable and inclusive society. These bonds offer a tangible way to channel capital towards initiatives that empower individuals, strengthen communities, and create a lasting positive impact.

Examples of Socially Responsible Bond Investments

The landscape of socially responsible bond investments is vast and diverse, encompassing a wide range of sectors and initiatives. Here are a few inspiring examples:

- The International Finance Corporation (IFC), a member of the World Bank Group, issued a social bond to support microfinance institutions in developing countries, providing access to financial services for underserved populations.

- The African Development Bank issued a green bond to finance renewable energy projects across the continent, contributing to Africa's sustainable development goals and reducing its carbon footprint.

- The City of Oslo issued a social bond to finance the construction of affordable housing units, addressing the pressing need for accessible housing in the Norwegian capital.

These examples, and countless others, illustrate the transformative power of bonds in driving positive social change. By aligning financial capital with social and environmental goals, these investments are creating a more sustainable, equitable, and prosperous future for all.

The Future of Africa: Bonds as Tools for Rapid Growth

Africa, a continent brimming with potential and rich in human intelligence and natural resources, stands on the cusp of a transformative era. Bonds, as instruments of development finance, can play a pivotal role in unlocking this potential and accelerating Africa's economic growth.

By channeling investments into critical infrastructure projects, such as roads, railways, and power plants, bonds can lay the foundations for sustainable development and attract further private sector investment. Moreover, green bonds can help finance renewable energy projects, reducing Africa's reliance on fossil fuels and mitigating the impact of climate change.

Social bonds, on the other hand, can address pressing social challenges, such as access to education, healthcare, and clean water. By empowering individuals and communities, these bonds can create a virtuous cycle of economic growth and social progress, paving the way for a more prosperous and inclusive Africa.

Bonds as Enablers of Reaching New Frontiers

As humanity sets its sights on exploring new frontiers, such as space travel and colonizing other planets, bonds can once again play a crucial role in financing these audacious endeavors. The immense capital requirements of such projects necessitate innovative financing mechanisms, and bonds, with their ability to mobilize large pools of capital, can provide the necessary financial fuel to propel us beyond the confines of our planet.

Imagine a future where bonds finance the construction of lunar bases, Martian colonies, and interstellar spacecraft. These investments, driven by the spirit of exploration and the pursuit of knowledge, would not only push the boundaries of human achievement but also create new industries, generate technological breakthroughs, and inspire generations to come.

In conclusion, bonds are no longer just financial instruments; they are catalysts for social impact, enablers of sustainable development, and the financial bedrock of our collective aspirations. By investing in bonds that align with our values and support projects that benefit society and the planet, we can create a more prosperous, equitable, and sustainable future for all.

Chapter 9: The Future of Bond Investing - Forging a Path to a Sustainable and Equitable World

As we stand at the crossroads of a new era, where environmental consciousness and social responsibility are reshaping the investment landscape, the future of bond investing shines brightly with promise and potential. Emerging trends, such as ESG investing and impact investing, are transforming the way investors allocate capital, seeking not only financial returns but also positive social and environmental outcomes. In this chapter, we will explore the exciting frontiers of bond investing and envision a future where finance serves as a catalyst for addressing global challenges and building a more sustainable and equitable world.

ESG Investing: Aligning Values with Investments

Environmental, Social, and Governance (ESG) investing is a rapidly growing movement that integrates environmental, social, and governance factors into investment analysis and decision-making. Investors are increasingly recognizing that companies with strong ESG performance are not only more likely to be sustainable in the long run but also more attractive to consumers, employees, and regulators.

In the bond market, this trend is manifested in the growing popularity of green bonds, social bonds, and sustainability-linked bonds. These instruments enable investors to support projects and initiatives that promote environmental sustainability, social progress, and responsible corporate governance. By incorporating ESG factors into their bond portfolios, investors can align their financial goals with their values, contributing to a more sustainable and equitable world.

Impact Investing: Measuring the Ripple Effect

Impact investing takes ESG investing a step further by actively seeking to measure and report the social and environmental impact of investments. Impact investors are not content with simply avoiding harm; they strive to generate positive outcomes that can be quantified and verified.

In the bond market, this trend is reflected in the emergence of impact bonds, which tie the financial returns of the bond to the achievement of specific social or environmental targets. For example, an impact bond might finance a program to reduce recidivism rates among former prisoners, with the bond's coupon payments linked to the program's success in achieving this goal.

Impact investing offers a powerful tool for addressing complex social and environmental challenges. By linking financial returns to measurable outcomes, impact bonds incentivize innovation, efficiency, and accountability, ensuring that capital is deployed effectively to create lasting positive change.

Addressing Global Challenges: Bonds as Agents of Change

The world faces a daunting array of challenges, from climate change and inequality to poverty and conflict. Bond investments, with their ability to mobilize large pools of capital and finance transformative projects, have the potential to play a pivotal role in addressing these global issues.

Green bonds can finance the transition to renewable energy, reducing carbon emissions and mitigating the impact of climate change. Social bonds can support initiatives that promote education, healthcare, and economic development, empowering individuals and communities to break the cycle of poverty. Impact bonds can foster innovation and drive efficiency in addressing social and environmental challenges.

By investing in bonds that support these critical initiatives, individuals and institutions can become agents of change, contributing to a more sustainable, equitable, and prosperous world.

The Path Forward: A Shared Vision

The future of bond investing is bright with possibilities. As ESG investing and impact investing continue to gain momentum, bonds will increasingly serve as vehicles for positive change, aligning financial goals with social and environmental values. The potential of bond investments to address global challenges is immense, and by embracing this opportunity, we can forge a path towards a more sustainable and equitable future for all.

Let us envision a world where financial markets are not just engines of wealth creation but also powerful forces for good. Let us imagine a future where bonds finance the transition to clean energy, empower communities, and foster a more inclusive and just society. This is the future of bond investing, and together, we can make it a reality.

Conclusion: Embark on a Voyage of Prosperity and Impact with Mayflower-Plymouth

As we conclude our exploration of the vast and dynamic world of bond investing, let us reflect on the transformative power of these financial instruments. From financing critical infrastructure projects to empowering communities and driving social progress, bonds have proven their ability to generate wealth and create a lasting positive impact on the world.

A Call to Action: Partner with Mayflower-Plymouth

For discerning investors seeking a trusted partner to navigate the complexities of the global bond market, Mayflower-Plymouth stands ready to guide you on your journey to financial success. Our unwavering commitment to Permaculture Investing principles in the Bond market ensures that your investments are not only profitable but also contribute to a more sustainable and equitable future.

By partnering with Mayflower-Plymouth, you gain access to a wealth of expertise and experience, honed through years of navigating the ever-changing tides of the bond market. Our team of seasoned professionals, armed with a deep understanding of global economic trends and a passion for responsible investing, will work tirelessly to tailor a bond portfolio that aligns with your unique financial goals and values.

Whether you are a seasoned investor seeking to diversify your portfolio or a newcomer eager to embark on your investment journey, Mayflower-Plymouth offers a range of investment options and personalized guidance to help you achieve your aspirations. Together, we can build a bond portfolio that not only generates consistent returns but also leaves a lasting legacy of positive change.

The Power of Bonds: A Force for Good

As we have explored throughout this book, bonds are more than just financial instruments; they are catalysts for progress, enablers of dreams, and builders of a better world. From the majestic bridges that connect communities to the renewable energy projects that power our future, bond investments have the potential to transform lives and shape the destiny of nations.

Let us embrace the power of bonds, not just as a means of generating wealth, but as a force for good. Let us invest with purpose, aligning our financial goals with our values and contributing to a more sustainable, equitable, and prosperous world.

The journey of bond investing is a lifelong endeavor, filled with opportunities for growth, learning, and impact. As you embark on this exciting path, remember that every investment you make has the potential to create a ripple effect, shaping the world around you and leaving a lasting legacy for generations to come.

Mayflower-Plymouth stands ready to be your trusted partner on this journey, guiding you towards financial success and empowering you to make a positive difference in the world. Together, let us unleash the full potential of bond investing and build a brighter future for all.

www.ingramcontent.com/pod-product-compliance
Lightning Source LLC
Chambersburg PA
CBHW072203170526
45158CB00004BB/1749